Tastes&Flavors
of **KAUA'I**

Tastes&Flavors
of KAUA'I

MUTUAL PUBLISHING

ISBN 1-56647-765-4
Library of Congress Catalog Card Number: 2005937654

Photographs on page 13, 14, 42, 50, 62, 71, flap and back cover (top right)
by Ray Wong
All other photographs © Douglas Peebles

Design by Wanni

First Printing, February 2006
1 2 3 4 5 6 7 8 9

Mutual Publishing, LLC
1215 Center Street, Suite 210
Honolulu, Hawai‘i 96816
Ph: 808-732-1709 / Fax: 808-734-4094
E-mail: mutual@mutualpublishing.com
www.mutualpublishing.com

Printed in China

TABLE OF CONTENTS

Desserts

Beverages & Drinks

Glossary

INTRODUCTION

Kaua'i, home of countless waterfalls, emerald valleys, and serene beaches, offers a natural —even spiritual—oasis for all who immerse themselves in its lush gardens and breathe its air

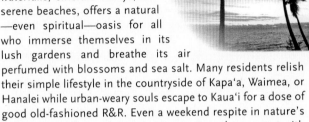

perfumed with blossoms and sea salt. Many residents relish their simple lifestyle in the countryside of Kapa'a, Waimea, or Hanalei while urban-weary souls escape to Kaua'i for a dose of good old-fashioned R&R. Even a weekend respite in nature's wonderland offers a chance to rejuvenate and reconnect with all things earthy and pure.

In much the same way, anyone can easily lose oneself in the culinary delights of this quaint tropical paradise. Kaua'i's slower pace of life gives birth to the sumptuous cooking and feasting of slow food: Kaua'i Sunrise papayas (sweeter, juicier, and redder than most), fresh herbs, avocadoes, and exotic fruits such as rambutan, rose and mountain apples, even the unique low-acid, white Sugarloaf pineapple that is rarer these days but still spottily available. Visitors, especially, will be pleasantly surprised to discover that seasons do exist on Kaua'i such as asparagus season in the fall and plum season in the summer. Of course, year-round produce colorful as a rainbow faithfully fills roadside stands and farmers' markets—a weekly display that reflects not only the local farming activities that are thriving all over Kaua'i but also the discerning palates of island people who love to eat.

Eating together, whether in daily ritual or in celebration, is the Hawaiian way of expressing love, friendship, and aloha. The spread of a lūʻau or a potluck gathering—where everything from freshly-pounded poi to guava spareribs brings family, friends, and even strangers together in camaraderie—signifies the sharing of a meal. Very often, the pleasure of eating also springs from the memories of a particular place that certain foods conjure. *Tastes & Flavors of Kauaʻi* promises to deliciously transport you recipe after recipe back to Kauaʻi, where the fish tastes like the sea and the fruits and vegetables burst with the colors of paradise.

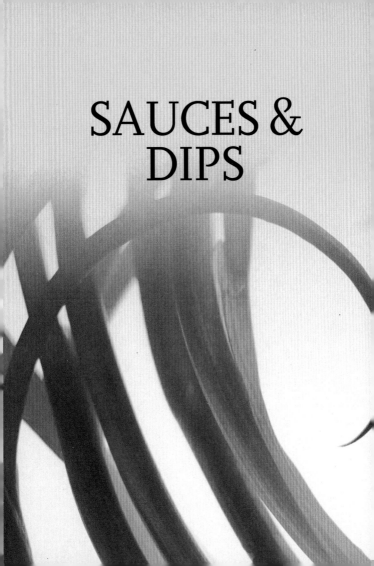

SAUCES & DIPS

Bata Yaki Sauce

Makes about 4 cups

3/4 cup sugar
1 tablespoon + 1 teaspoon mayonnaise
1 cup soy sauce
1 cup sake
1 cup mirin
2 tablespoons + 2 teaspoons sesame oil
1 tablespoon garlic, crushed
1 tablespoon fresh ginger, grated
Dash of pepper
1 tablespoon lemon juice
Green onion slices

Heat all ingredients, except green onion, on low heat for
20 minutes. Serve with beef stir-fried in butter. Use onion to
garnish.

—*Recipe by* Galyn Wong

Spinach Dip

1 box thawed frozen spinach, drained and chopped
1 teaspoon garlic, chopped
1 cup mayonnaise
1 cup sour cream or yogurt
1 package of leek soup mix or Ranch dressing

Mix together all ingredients and refrigerate 1 hour.

Options for display: Use a round loaf of bread, cut out a hole in the top of the bread and scoop out most of the inside. Freeze the bread for one hour. Fill the bread with the Spinach Dip and serve with an assortment of vegetables and/or chips and crackers.

—*Recipe by* Galyn Wong

JAMS &
DRESSINGS

Hanapēpē Papaya Seed Dressing

Makes about 1 quart

1 cup white wine vinegar
1/3 cup lemon juice
3/4 cup honey
1/2 cup fresh parsley
1 teaspoon paprika
1-1/2 teaspoons salt
4 cloves garlic
1 teaspoon fresh-ground pepper
2 whole papayas, skinned
3 cups canola oil

Combine all ingredients in blender with oil on top. Process until well blended. Add 2 cups of water; blend until well combined. Serve over fresh island greens.

Kōke'e Plum Jam

Makes about 4 pints

4 pounds (52 to 58) ripe plums, washed and drained
1-1/2 cups water
1 cup sugar to each cup of pulp

Remove stems and damaged spots from plums. Add water and boil gently for 10 to 15 minutes, stirring occasionally, until fruit is soft. Strain to remove pits and skins. Measure pulp and add equal amount of sugar; mix well and cook rapidly until it gives a good jelly test—221°F to 222°F. Remove scum during cooking. Put hot jam into sterilized jars and seal.

Notes: The only variety of plum grown extensively at higher elevations in Hawai'i, like Kōke'e, is Methley. When fully ripe, the plum is best eaten as a fresh fruit.

SOUPS &
SALADS

Kaua'i Onion Soup

Serves 6 to 8

1/4 cup olive oil
2 large Kaua'i sweet onions, sliced thin
    (may substitute Maui or Vidalia)
3 cups chicken broth or stock
3 cups beef broth or stock
6 black peppercorns
3 cloves
1 bay leaf
1/4 cup dry sherry wine
Salt and pepper to taste

Toppings
Toasted croutons and grated Gruyère cheese

In heavy soup pot, heat the olive oil until smoking. Add the sliced onions; spread out but do not stir. Allow the onions to start to caramelize then stir to expose all sides. Add the stocks. Make a small sachet using cheesecloth and tie it up tightly with the peppercorns, cloves, and bay leaf inside. Add to the soup; bring to a boil and turn down heat to simmer slowly for about 25 to 30 minutes. Add sherry wine. Adjust the seasoning with salt and pepper. Place ovenproof soup bowls or crocks on baking sheet. Ladle hot soup into bowls and top each with toasted croutons and sprinkle with cheese. Broil or bake at 450°F until cheese is melted and starting to brown. Serve immediately.

—*Recipe by* Executive Chef Mark D. Secker

Po'ipū Seafood Chowder

Serves 6 to 8

4 strips bacon, diced
1 onion, chopped
2 stalks celery, chopped
1 cup white wine
2 potatoes, peeled and diced
2 cups Fish Stock (recipe follows)
1/2 pound firm white fish (sea bass, mahimahi, ono, 'ahi)
    or smoked marlin, cubed
1/2 pound scallops, cut in half
1 teaspoon salt
1/2 teaspoon white pepper
Pinch of thyme
1 cup heavy cream
Chopped fresh parsley

Sauté bacon in heavy stockpot. Remove bacon and set aside, reserve drippings. Sauté onion and celery until onions are translucent. Add wine, potatoes, and Fish Stock. Cover and simmer over low heat until reduced by half and potatoes are tender. Stir in bacon, fish, scallops, salt, white pepper, and thyme. Cover and cook until fish flakes easily when tested with a fork, almost 8 minutes. Stir in heavy cream and heat thoroughly. Garnish with parsley to serve.

continued on next page

Fish Stock

2 pounds fish bones
1 carrot, chopped
1 onion, chopped
2 stalks celery, chopped
1 cup white wine
1-inch piece fresh ginger, crushed
1-1/4 teaspoons salt
1/4 teaspoon white pepper

Rinse fish bones and combine in a large stockpot with vegetables, wine, ginger, salt, and pepper; add water to cover. Bring to a boil; reduce heat and simmer for 45 minutes. Strain. Store in refrigerator until ready to use.

—*Recipe by* Chef Sam Choy

Crab Potato Pasta Salad

Serves 6 to 8

8 ounces elbow macaroni or other similar pasta, cooked
5 or 6 hard-cooked eggs, chopped
3 large cooked potatoes, diced
2 cups mayonnaise
8 ounces imitation crab, shredded
1/4 cup diced celery
1/4 cup grated carrots
1/2 cup frozen peas, defrosted and drained
5 or 6 black olives, chopped
Salt and pepper to taste

Combine all ingredients and toss to mix well. Chill well before serving.

—Recipe by Joanne Fujita

Spinach Salad with Oranges and Warm Goat Cheese

Serves 4

3 small navel oranges
6 ounces fresh mild goat cheese (preferably in log form)
1/3 cup macadamia nuts, finely chopped
1 teaspoon whole-grain mustard
1 teaspoon white wine vinegar
1/2 teaspoon kosher salt
Pinch of sugar
2 tablespoons extra virgin olive oil
1 pound spinach, trimmed
1 small red onion, sliced into thin rings
8 slices apple-smoked bacon, cooked crisp

Preheat oven to 350°F. Cut peel and remove white pith from oranges with a small sharp knife. Working over a sieve set over a bowl, cut orange sections free from membranes, letting sections drop into sieve. Cut goat cheese into fourths and gently form into a disk; dip into macadamia nuts and coat all over. Bake on a small baking sheet in middle of oven until heated through, about 5 minutes. Measure out 1 tablespoon orange juice from bowl and whisk together with mustard, vinegar, salt, and sugar in a large bowl. Add oil and whisk until blended. Add spinach, onion, bacon, and orange sections to dressing and toss well. Season with pepper. Divide among 4 salad plates and serve with goat cheese disk to each salad.

Grilled Kaua'i Sweet Onions and Vine-Ripened Tomatoes

Serves 1

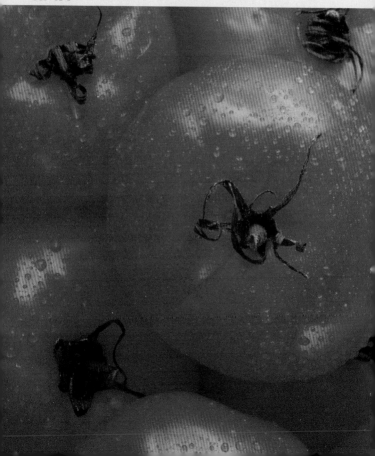

4 slices Kaua'i sweet onions
Marinated Tomatoes (see recipe below)
Black Pepper Balsamic Vinaigrette (see recipe below)

Slice onions 1/2 inch thick. Marinate in Black Pepper
Balsamic Vinaigrette for 15 minutes. Grill onions until soft.
Serve at room temperature. Arrange on plate artfully with
marinated tomatoes and dress with Black Pepper Balsamic
Vinaigrette.

Black Pepper Balsamic Vinaigrette
1/2 cup balsamic vinegar
1/4 cup rice wine vinegar
2 tablespoons freshly ground black pepper
1/3 cup sugar
2/3 cup olive oil
Kosher salt to taste

In a saucepan combine balsamic vinegar, rice wine vinegar,
and pepper. Bring to a boil and reduce by one-half. In another
saucepan bring sugar and water to a boil. Add oil and adjust
seasoning to taste.

continued on next page

Marinated Tomatoes
4 slices vine-ripened tomatoes
2 teaspoons minced garlic
1 teaspoon minced ginger
2 teaspoons chopped basil
2 tablespoons olive oil

Cut tomatoes into 1/2-inch thick slices. Blend together
remaining ingredients and pour over tomatoes to marinate.

—*Recipe by* David Boucher, Hyatt Regency Kaua'i

ENTRÉES

Pesto on Pasta

Serves 4 to 6

2 cups fresh basil, firmly packed
1/3 cup macadamia nuts
3 cloves garlic, peeled
1/2 cup Parmesan cheese, freshly grated
1/2 cup extra virgin olive oil, or more if needed
Salt and pepper to taste

1 quart water
1 pound bowtie pasta
1 teaspoon salt

Garnish
Basil leaves

In a food processor, puree the basil, macadamia nuts, and garlic. Blend in Parmesan cheese. Add olive oil slowly on low speed. Process for 30 seconds or until mixture reaches consistency of rough pasta. Pesto can be kept by drizzling a thin layer of olive oil over the top and storing in a covered container in the refrigerator for up to 2 weeks.

Bring water to rolling boil; add pasta to boiling water and cook until pasta is al dente, stirring occasionally. Drain and toss pasta with pesto and garnish with basil leaves, if desired.

Notes: Substitute almonds, walnuts, or pine nuts for the macadamia nuts. A tablespoon of other herbs can be used with the basil, such as parsley sprigs, dill weed, chives, rosemary, oregano, marjoram, or thyme. This can be served over steaks, potatoes, in soups, or with scrambled eggs.

If freezing pesto sauce, add nuts and cheese after thawing.

Paniolo Steak with Kaua'i Onion Rings

Serves 2

2 (8-ounce) rib steaks
2 cloves garlic, chopped
Salt and pepper to taste

Grill outdoors over charcoal or gas barbecue grill to desired doneness. Serve with Kaua'i Onion Rings.

Kaua'i Onion Rings
1 cup buttermilk
Dash of Tabasco®
4 large Kaua'i onions, cut in 1/4-inch rings
1 cup flour
Oil for deep-frying

In a shallow dish, mix buttermilk with Tabasco®. Dip onion slices into milk mixture. Then dredge onions in flour, shake off any excess. Gently place onions into hot oil and fry until golden brown. Drain on paper towels. Serve hot.

—*Recipe by* Galyn Wong

Shrimp-Eggplant Stir-Fry

Serves 4

2 tablespoons salad oil
8 whole extra jumbo shrimp (16 to 20 count),
　　peeled and deveined
2 large eggplants, sliced into 1-inch chunks
1 tablespoon minced fresh garlic
1 tablespoon peeled and minced fresh ginger
1 teaspoon red chili pepper flakes
1 tablespoon oyster sauce
1 tablespoon soy sauce
1 cup chicken broth
Pinch of salt
Pinch of pepper
2 tablespoons cornstarch mixed with 2 tablespoons water

Heat oil in wok over high heat. Add shrimp and cook about 1 minute. Remove shrimp and repeat with eggplant. Add garlic, ginger, chili flakes, and shrimp; sauté another minute. Add the oyster sauce, soy sauce, chicken stock, salt, and pepper. Cook about 2 minutes or until shrimp are just cooked and eggplant is tender. Stir in cornstarch mixture and let it come to a boil. Serve over noodles or rice.

Notes: Eggplant may take longer than 1 minute to cook.

—*Recipe by* Chef Sam Choy

Stir-Fried Beef with Snow Peas

Serves 4

1 pound lean beef, thinly sliced against grain
2 teaspoons cornstarch
1 teaspoon sugar
2 teaspoons oyster sauce
1 tablespoon soy sauce
1 tablespoon sweet vermouth
3 tablespoons oil
1/2-inch piece of fresh ginger, sliced
3/4 pound snow peas, cleaned
1 cup chicken broth
Salt and pepper to taste

Thickening Mixture
1 teaspoon sugar
1 tablespoon cornstarch
1 tablespoon water

Combine cornstarch, sugar, oyster sauce, soy sauce, and vermouth, and massage into meat for 1 minute. Let stand 2 to 3 minutes to marinate. Heat 1 tablespoon oil on medium-high heat in wok or sauté pan. Stir-fry ginger 1 to 2 minutes. Add snow peas and stir-fry 1 to 2 minutes more. Remove and set aside. Add remaining 2 tablespoons of oil and stir-fry beef on medium-high heat until beef begins to brown; add broth, peas, and ginger and bring to a boil. Season with salt and pepper to taste. Add Thickening Mixture; return to a boil and stir until thickened. Serve with hot steamed rice.

—*Recipe by* Chef Sam Choy

Honey-Baked Chicken

Serves 4 to 6

2 pounds of chicken thighs
1 cup honey
3 tablespoons rosemary, crushed
1 tablespoon garlic powder
1 teaspoon salt
1/2 teaspoon pepper
1/2 teaspoon crushed thyme sprigs
1 teaspoon paprika

Mix together all ingredients; pour over chicken in a foil-lined baking dish. Bake at 400°F for 40 minutes, or until done, basting occasionally.

—*Recipe by* Galyn Wong

Barbecue Chicken

Serves 8

5 pounds chicken pieces

Sauce
1/3 cup ketchup
1/3 cup soy sauce
1/4 cup brown sugar, packed
3 tablespoons sherry
1 piece ginger root, crushed
1 clove garlic, crushed

Arrange chicken, skin side up, on rack of broiler pan. Broil 6 to 8 inches from heat for 10 minutes on each side. Combine sauce ingredients and mix well; baste chicken and continue broiling for 10 more minutes on each side, or until done, basting frequently with sauce.

—*Recipe by* Galyn Wong

Seared Opah

Serves 2

Marinade
1 tablespoon minced fresh ginger
1 teaspoon minced garlic
1 tablespoon chopped cilantro
Pinch of salt
Pinch of pepper

4 opah (moonfish) fillets (3 ounces each)
2 tablespoons canola oil
1/2 cup julienne carrots and zucchini
2 fresh shiitake mushrooms, softened and sliced
2 teaspoons soy sauce
1 tablespoon oyster sauce

Combine Marinade ingredients and marinate fish 5 minutes. Heat oil in a heavy skillet and cook fillets about 2 minutes on each side or until brown. Transfer fish to a warm plate. Stir-fry carrots and zucchini in skillet about 2 minutes. Arrange 2 opah fillets on a serving plate and top with cooked carrots and zucchini. Place remaining 2 opah fillets on top. Cook mushrooms, soy sauce, and oyster sauce in skillet and cook about 1 minute; pour over fish to serve.

—*Recipe by* Chef Sam Choy

Shrimp Scampi with Dill Cream Sauce over Taro and Pasta

Serves 4 to 6

Marinade
1 tablespoon garlic, minced
1 tablespoon olive oil
Salt and pepper to taste

2 pounds large shrimp (16 to 20 count),
    peeled and deveined
Flour (enough to dust shrimp)
2 tablespoons olive oil
2 cloves garlic, minced
2 cups cooked taro, diced into large chunks
2 tablespoons butter
1 pound linguine, cooked and drained
1 tablespoon soy sauce
5 cups heavy cream (may need more)
2 tablespoons fresh dill, minced
Salt and pepper to taste
1/4 cup grated Parmesan cheese

Mix Marinade ingredients and marinate shrimp for 15 to 20 minutes. Dust shrimp with flour and sear quickly in 2 tablespoons olive oil on medium-high heat for about 1 minute. Remove from heat and set aside (shrimp will be raw on the inside). Sauté garlic with taro in butter. Add linguine, soy sauce, and heavy cream, and bring to a quick boil. Reduce heat and continue simmering until thick, about 3 or 4 minutes. Add shrimp and dill and adjust seasoning with salt and pepper. Cook for another minute or until shrimp are done, then fold in grated Parmesan cheese. Serve in pasta bowls with fresh baked garlic bread and tossed greens.

If the pasta absorbs a lot of liquid, you may need to add a little more cream. If so, continue to cook until reduced to desired consistency.

—Recipe by Chef Sam Choy

Līhuʻe Saimin

Serves 4

2 packages (9-1/2 ounces each) fresh saimin (noodles)

Kakejiru (broth)
8 cups water
2 packages (2-1/2 teaspoons each) dashi-no-moto
(instant stock granules)
1/4 cup shoyu
3 tablespoons mirin (sweet rice wine)

Garnishes
Kamaboko (fishcake) slices
Fried egg strips
Ajitsuke nori (seasoned seaweed)
Minced green onion
Char siu (sweet roasted pork) slices
Roast pork slices
Luncheon meat slices, julienne

Cook saimin following package directions. Pour hot noodles into a colander and rinse well under cold running water; drain. When ready to serve, reheat noodles by pouring hot boiling water over; drain. Place hot noodles into warmed individual bowls.

To prepare Kakejiru: combine all ingredients and bring to a boil, lower heat and simmer 5 minutes. Ladle about 1-1/2 cups over each serving of hot noodles and garnish as desired to serve.

'Ono Oven-Braised Ribs

Serves 4

3 pounds meaty country-style pork spareribs,
    cut in pieces
3 tablespoons soy sauce
1 teaspoon salt
Dash of pepper

Sauce
1 cup syrup-packed pineapple chunks, drained
1/4 cup brown sugar, packed
1/3 cup ketchup
1/3 cup vinegar
3 tablespoons soy sauce
2 teaspoons grated fresh ginger
1 clove garlic, minced

Garnishes
Pineapple chunks
Chopped green onion

Rub spareribs all over with 3 tablespoons of the soy sauce, salt, and pepper. Place ribs, meat side up, in a foil-lined shallow baking or roasting pan, and cover with foil or baking-pan lid. Bake 20 to 25 minutes at 450°F. Drain off fat. Combine Sauce ingredients; pour over ribs. Bake at 350°F for 1 hour, or until tender, basting occasionally. Garnish with pineapple chunks and green onions to serve.

—Recipe by Chef Sam Choy

Coconut Macadamia Crusted Shrimp with Guava Sauce

Serves 4

1 cup coconut flakes
1 cup roasted macadamia nuts, crushed
2-1/2 cups panko (Japanese-style crispy bread crumbs)
24 pieces shrimp (21 to 25 pieces per pound),
    shelled and deveined
1 cup all-purpose flour
3 eggs, beaten
1 quart vegetable oil for frying
Salt and pepper to taste

Mix coconut flakes, macadamia nuts, and panko together. Set aside. Bread the shrimp in flour, egg, and then in coconut flake–macadamia nut–panko mixture. Season with salt and pepper. Deep-fry in hot oil until golden brown. Drain on paper towels and serve with Guava Sauce.

continued on next page

Guava Sauce (Makes about 4 cups)

3/4 cup ketchup
3/4 cup white wine vinegar
3/4 cup water
2 teaspoons Aloha soy sauce
3/4 cup granulated sugar
1/2 cup frozen guava concentrate, undiluted
1 clove garlic, minced
1/4 teaspoon hot pepper sauce
1/4 cup pineapple juice
1/4 cup cornstarch
3 tablespoons water

In a medium saucepan, combine all Guava Sauce ingredients except cornstarch and water. Blend well then bring to a boil. Make paste of cornstarch and water. Reduce heat and simmer 1 to 2 minutes, stirring frequently until thickened.

—*Recipe by* Chef Sam Choy

Mahimahi Crunch

Serves 2

1 tablespoon fresh cilantro, chopped
Salt and pepper to taste
1-1/2 cups brown sugar, packed
1 clove garlic, minced
1 tablespoon fresh ginger, minced
3 tablespoons salad oil
4 mahimahi fillets (3 ounces each)

Vegetable Sauté
2 tablespoons butter
1 Kaua'i sweet onion, julienne
1/4 cup carrots, julienne
1/4 cup zucchini, julienne
1 cup sugar snap peas
1 tablespoon soy sauce
2 teaspoons oyster sauce

Mix together cilantro, salt, pepper, brown sugar, garlic, and ginger. Rub mixture evenly into the mahimahi fillets to coat, and let stand for about 5 minutes. Meanwhile, heat oil in a

continued on next page

heavy skillet. Cook mahimahi fillets in butter for about 2 minutes on each side or until brown. In separate skillet, sauté onions in butter for 30 seconds over medium-high heat. Add carrots, zucchini, and sugar snap peas, and sauté for additional 2 minutes. Add soy sauce and oyster sauce; cook for 1 minute longer. Remove from heat and place vegetables around the mahimahi to serve.

—*Recipe by* Chef Sam Choy

DESSERTS

Liliko'i *(Passion Fruit)* Bars

Makes about 24 to 30 bars

Crust
1 cup flour
1 teaspoon baking soda
2-1/4 cups quick-cooking rolled oats
1 cup brown sugar, packed
1 cup melted butter or margarine

Filling
4 eggs
1-1/2 cups sugar
1/2 cup liliko'i (passion fruit) juice
1/2 teaspoon fresh lemon juice
1/2 cup flour
1 teaspoon baking powder
1/8 teaspoon salt
Confectioners' sugar

To prepare Crust: Mix flour, baking soda, rolled oats, and brown sugar together; add butter or margarine. Toss to blend thoroughly. Press into lightly greased 9 x 13 x 2-inch pan, building up sides. Bake at 350°F for 20 to 25 minutes. Set aside.

To prepare Filling: Beat eggs; add sugar, passion fruit juice, and lemon juice. Sift flour, baking powder, and salt together; add to liquid mixture. Pour over crust and bake at 350°F for 25 to 30 minutes. Cool and sprinkle with confectioners' sugar. Cut into bars.

Hanalei Poi Mochi

Makes 6 dozen

1 pound fresh poi
1 cup sugar
1 box (1 pound) mochiko
3/4 cup coconut milk or water
1/2 teaspoon vanilla extract
1/2 cup coconut flakes, optional
1 quart salad oil for frying

Mix all ingredients together (except for salad oil). Drop dough by teaspoonfuls into oil heated to 375°F. Fry until golden brown. Drain on paper towels. Cool.

Mango Bread

Makes 2 (9 x 5-inch) loaves

2 cups all-purpose flour
2 teaspoons baking soda
1 teaspoon baking powder
2 teaspoons cinnamon
3 eggs, well beaten
3/4 cup canola oil
1-1/4 cups granulated sugar
2 cups fresh mango, peeled and diced
1/2 cup raisins
1/4 cup chopped macadamia nuts or walnuts

Preheat oven to 350°F. Grease and flour two 9 x 5-inch loaf pans. Sift together the flour, baking soda, baking powder, and cinnamon. In a large mixing bowl, combine the eggs, oil, and sugar; mix in dry ingredients and blend well. Fold in mango, raisins, and nuts. Pour batter into prepared loaf pans and bake for 45 to 60 minutes, or until the bread is golden brown and a toothpick inserted in the center comes out clean.

Let loaves cool in the pan for 10 to 15 minutes, then unmold and let cool completely on racks. Drizzle with icing, if desired.

Hanalei Poi Bread

Makes 2 (9 x 5-inch) loaves

1 pound bag fresh poi
1/2 cup water
2 cups flour
1 cup sugar
2 teaspoons cinnamon
1/4 teaspoon nutmeg
2 teaspoons baking powder
1 teaspoon salt
3 eggs, slightly beaten
1 cup vegetable oil
2 teaspoons vanilla extract
1/3 cup chopped nuts
1/4 cup shredded coconut
1/2 cup raisins

Mix poi with water; blend well. In a large bowl, combine flour, sugar, cinnamon, nutmeg, baking powder, and salt. In a separate bowl, combine eggs, oil, and vanilla; add to flour mixture. Stir in poi; add nuts, coconut, and raisins. Pour into 2 greased and floured 9 x 5 inch loaf pans, and bake at 350°F approximately 45 minutes, or until toothpick inserted in center comes out clean.

—*Originally appeared in* Ethnic Foods of Hawai'i

Papaya or Mango Sorbet

Makes 6 cups

4 ripe mangoes or 3 ripe papayas
1 cup Simple Syrup (recipe follows)
3 tablespoons fresh lime juice, or to taste

Wash and dry fruit. Peel, seed, and cut fruit coarsely. Place fruit in blender, add syrup and lime juice, and purée until smooth. Freeze fruit purée in an ice cream maker, and follow manufacturer's instructions.

Simple Syrup (Makes 4-1/2 cups)
3 cups sugar
3 cups water

In a saucepan bring sugar and water to a boil, stirring constantly. Boil until sugar is completely dissolved. Cool syrup. Syrup may be made ahead, covered, and chilled. This syrup will keep at least 2 months in the refrigerator.

—*Recipe by* Joanne Fujita

Kōloa Pao Doce
(Portuguese Sweet Bread)
Makes 4 loaves

2 packages active dry yeast
1/2 cup warm potato water
2 cups sugar
1 cup mashed potatoes
1/8 teaspoon ground ginger, optional
1-1/2 teaspoons salt
1/2 cup milk, scalded
1/2 cup butter or margarine, melted
8 to 10 cups all-purpose flour
6 eggs, beaten

Sprinkle yeast over potato water. Stir in 1/4 cup of sugar,
potatoes, and ginger; cover and let rise until doubled. Add salt
to scalded milk; cool to lukewarm. In a small mixing bowl,
gradually beat in remaining sugar; stir into yeast mixture.
Add butter and mix well. Stir in 2 cups flour, then milk.
Add 2 more cups of flour; beat for 5 minutes. Stir in enough
of remaining flour to make a stiff dough.

Place dough on a lightly floured board and knead in remaining flour until dough is smooth and elastic, about 8 to 10 minutes. Place dough in a large greased bowl, turning once to grease top. Cover; let rise until doubled, about 1 hour. Grease four 9 x 5 x 3-inch loaf pans. Divide dough into fourths on lightly floured board. Shape each fourth into a loaf; place in prepared pans. Cover; let rise until doubled, about 1 hour. Brush loaves with beaten egg. Bake at 325°F for 45 to 50 minutes, or until golden brown. Cool.

Kaua'i Coffee Brûlée

Serves 6 to 8

4 egg yolks
1/3 cup sugar
2 teaspoons coarsely ground Kaua'i espresso coffee beans
2 cups heavy cream
1 teaspoon vanilla extract
3/4 cup sugar, divided

In a medium bowl, beat egg yolks and 1/3 cup sugar with whisk until pale and thick. Set aside. In another bowl, combine coffee with 1/2 cup cream and whisk until smooth then add remaining cream and vanilla; whisk until well blended. Fold egg yolk mixture into coffee–cream mixture. Pour mixture into 6 ramekins and place in 2-inch deep baking pan. Add enough hot water to pan to come half way up the sides of the ramekins. Bake at 325°F for about 30 to 40 minutes or until custard is set around the edges but still a little loose in the center. Remove from baking pan; cool then refrigerate until cold, about 1 to 2 hours.

When ready to serve, sprinkle tops of custards with 2 tablespoons sugar. Caramelize sugar with a small blowtorch or place under the broiler until sugar caramelizes, taking care not to let them burn. Serve immediately.

Kaua'i Coffee Ice Cream Pie

Serves 8

3 pints vanilla ice cream
1-1/2 cups heavy cream
3/4 cup macadamia nuts, coarsely chopped
2 tablespoons coffee liqueur
2 tablespoons instant coffee
9-inch baked pastry shell

Meringue
4 egg whites
1/4 teaspoon cream of tartar
1/2 cup sugar
1/2 teaspoon vanilla extract

Garnish
Maraschino cherries (optional)

Soften 1 pint ice cream in a medium size bowl. Beat 1/2 cup heavy cream in a small chilled bowl until stiff. Fold into softened ice cream along with nuts and liqueur. If very soft, place in freezer until mixture holds its shape. Soften remaining 2 pints ice cream in large bowl. Stir instant coffee into remaining heavy cream; beat until stiff and fold into remaining softened ice cream. Spread 2/3 of coffee mixture in baked pastry shell. Make a depression in center.

Spoon macadamia mixture into center. Mound remaining coffee mixture on top. Freeze overnight or until firm.

Beat egg whites and cream of tartar until foamy. Beat in sugar one tablespoon at a time until meringue forms soft peaks. Add cream of tartar and beat on high speed until peaks are stiff and glassy but not dry. Beat in vanilla and immediately swirl meringue decoratively with back of spoon. Cover ice cream filling with meringue, anchoring it to edge of crust. Bake at 500°F for 2 to 3 minutes or until meringue is slightly browned. Serve immediately. Now garnish with maraschino cherries, if desired.

Kaua'i Mac Nut Brittle

Makes about 6 dozen pieces

1-1/2 teaspoons baking soda
1 teaspoon vanilla extract
1 cup water
1-1/2 cups sugar
1 cup light corn syrup
2 cups macadamia nuts, chopped
1/4 cup butter

Mix baking soda, vanilla, and 1 teaspoon water. Set aside. Combine water, sugar, and corn syrup in 3-quart saucepan; cook over medium heat, stirring occasionally, to 275°F on candy thermometer. Stir in nuts and cook until 300°F, using candy thermometer, or until small amount of mixture dropped into very cold water separates into hard brittle threads. Remove from heat; add butter and baking soda mixture. Stir then pour onto greased cookie sheet and spread to about 1/4-inch thickness to cool. When cooled, break into pieces. Peanuts may be substituted for macadamia nuts. If peanuts are used, reduce first temperature to 225°F.

—*Recipe by* Carol Cummings

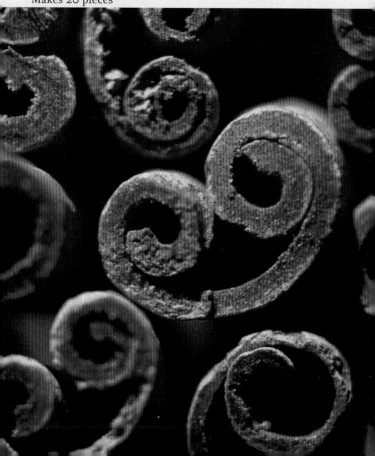

Mango Phyllo Triangles

Makes 20 pieces

4 cups sliced mangoes
3/4 cup granulated sugar (less for riper mangoes)
1/3 cup water
1 teaspoon lemon juice
1 teaspoon cinnamon
1/8 teaspoon freshly ground nutmeg
1 tablespoon tapioca
3 tablespoons cornstarch
3 tablespoons water
1 box phyllo pastry
1/2 cup (1 stick) butter, melted
Confectioners' sugar

Cook the first seven ingredients over medium-high heat,
stirring occasionally until it starts to boil. Mix cornstarch and
water together; add to mango mixture and stir well, cooking
until thickened. Let cool. Preheat oven to 350°F.

Follow defrosting instructions on phyllo box. Unroll phyllo.
With long side facing you, cut phyllo into four strips
approximately 4 x 12 inches in size. (Kitchen shears are very
helpful for this task.) Use caution, as phyllo is thin and very
fragile. Brush a 4 x 12-inch sheet with butter, top with another
sheet, and continue to butter and stack until you have three
layers. Butter the top sheet, too. Place a heaping tablespoon of
mango filling in one corner of the pastry. Fold into a triangle
(like folding a flag) and place on greased cookie sheet. Repeat
procedure with the rest of the pastry and filling. Bake at 350°F
for 15 to 20 minutes. Dust with confectioners' sugar.

—*Recipe by* Joanne Fujita

Kaua'i Shortbread Cookies

1/2 cup butter
1/2 cup shortening
1/2 cup sugar
2 cups flour
1/8 teaspoon salt
1/4 teaspoon vanilla extract

Cream butter and shortening together. Add sugar to the mix until light and fluffy. Add flour and salt; mix together; add vanilla and blend well. Shape into logs about 1-1/2 to 2-inches in diameter; refrigerate about 1 hour. Slice and place on lightly greased cookie sheet. Bake at 350°F for 12 to 15 minutes. Cool and store in sealed containers.

Garden Isle Liliko'i *(PassionFruit)* Chiffon Pie

Serves 6 to 8

1 tablespoon unflavored gelatin
1/4 cup cold water
4 eggs, separated
1 cup sugar
1/2 teaspoon salt
1/2 cup fresh liliko'i juice
1 teaspoon zest of lemon
1 baked 9-inch pastry shell
Sweetened whipped cream

Sprinkle gelatin over cold water; let stand 15 minutes to soften. Beat egg yolks in saucepan until thick; add 1/2 cup of the sugar, salt, and liliko'i juice; mix well. Cook, stirring constantly, over low heat until thickened, about 10 minutes. Add softened gelatin and stir until gelatin dissolves. Add lemon zest; refrigerate until slightly congealed. Meanwhile, beat egg whites until frothy, add remaining 1/2 cup of sugar slowly and continue beating until meringue is stiff. Fold cold gelatin mixture into meringue. Pour into baked pastry shell and refrigerate until firm, about 2 to 3 hours. Top with whipped cream to serve.

Kalāheo Carrot Cake

Serves 18 to 24

3 cups flour
1 teaspoon baking powder
1 teaspoon baking soda
1 teaspoon salt
1 teaspoon cinnamon
3 eggs, beaten
2 cups sugar
1-1/2 cups salad oil
2 teaspoons vanilla
1 can (8-1/4 ounces) crushed pineapple
2 cups grated carrots
1 cup chopped macadamia nuts

Butter Cream Cheese Frosting
1/4 cup butter, softened
8 ounces cream cheese
1-1/2 cups Confectioners' sugar
1 teaspoon vanilla extract

Sift together flour, baking powder, baking soda, salt, and cinnamon; set aside. Beat eggs, sugar, oil, and vanilla together; add pineapple, carrots, and nuts and stir to blend ingredients. Add dry ingredients to wet mixture. Pour into greased and floured 9 x 13-inch pan. Bake at 350°F for 45 to 50 minutes, or until cake tester inserted in center comes out clean. Cool well and frost with Butter Cream Cheese Frosting.

To prepare Butter Cream Cheese Frosting: Beat butter and cream cheese together until blended. Add remaining ingredients and beat until smooth. Frost cooled cake.

Banana Foster

Serves 4

1/2 cup butter
1/2 cup honey
1/2 cup brown sugar, packed
1/4 teaspoon ground cinnamon
1/8 teaspoon ground nutmeg
4 firm-ripe medium bananas, peeled and
    cut in half lengthwise
1/4 cup dark rum
Vanilla ice cream

In a large skillet melt butter. Stir in honey, brown sugar, cinnamon, and nutmeg; blend well. Place bananas, cut side down, and cook in skillet over low heat for 5 minutes; turn and cook another 3 to 5 minutes or until fork tender. Baste bananas well in the sauce. Turn off the heat (the pan should still be warm). Carefully add rum to skillet and warm for a few seconds; ignite with a long wooden match. Baste bananas in sauce and rum until flame goes out. Pour bananas into serving dish and top with vanilla ice cream.

Note: Be careful when igniting flame. If preferred, bananas can be made without the rum and igniting flames.

—Recipe by Jeffrey Lee

BEVERAGES &
DRINKS

Princeville Smoothie

Serves 1

1 ounce vodka
1 ounce orange juice
1 ounce cranberry juice
2 ounces strawberry puree
1 ounce Grenadine syrup
Ice

Garnishes
3 tablespoons whipped cream
1 maraschino cherry

Fill blender with ice to 1/3 full. Add ingredients and blend. Pour mixture into a Viva Grande glass, and top with whipped cream. Garnish with a maraschino cherry.

—*Recipe by* Chef Sam Choy

Kaua'i Fizz

Makes 1 gallon

1 (12-ounce) can frozen orange juice concentrate, thawed
1 (12-ounce) can frozen pineapple juice concentrate, thawed
1/4 cup lemon juice
2 bottles champagne, chilled
1 liter lemon-lime soda, chilled

Garnish
Orange slices

Mix juices together and chill. Just before serving, add
champagne and soda. Stir and garnish with floating orange
slices.

Mocha Punch

Makes 5 quarts

1 quart whipping cream
1/2 cup sugar
1-1/2 teaspoons vanilla extract
4 quarts strong Kaua'i coffee, chilled
1/4 cup chocolate syrup
1/4 cup coffee liqueur, optional
1/2 gallon vanilla ice cream

Garnish
Chocolate shavings

Whip cream until soft peaks form; add sugar and vanilla gradually and continue beating until stiff. Combine coffee, chocolate syrup, and liqueur. Spoon ice cream into large punch bowl and pour coffee mixture over. Top with whipped cream and garnish with chocolate shavings to serve.

Hanalei Coffee

Serves 4 to 6

1 slice lemon peel
1 slice orange peel
2 whole cloves
1 cinnamon stick
4 cubes sugar
1/4 teaspoon vanilla
1 cup brandy
2 cups very strong coffee

Place fruit peels, spices, sugar, vanilla, and brandy in the top pan of a chafing dish and heat. Place a lump of sugar in a ladle of brandy and ignite. When the brandy is blazing, lower the ladle slowly into the pan. Pour the coffee in and blend. When blaze has burned out serve at once in small demitasse cups.

GLOSSARY

A

'Ahi:
The Hawaiian name for both yellowfin and big-eye tuna. Often served in the Islands as sashimi (Japanese-style raw fish).

B

Bata Yaki sauce:
Cooking butter.

C

Cilantro:
A pungent flat-leaf herb resembling parsley; also called fresh coriander or Chinese parsley.

Coconut:
The fruit of the coconut tree featuring a hard, brown outer shell containing white meat on the inside. The liquid extracted from shredded coconut meat can be drank as milk or used in cooking.

G

Ginger:
Fresh ginger is a brown, fibrous, knobby rhizome. It keeps for long periods of time. To use, peel the brown skin and slice, chop, or purée.

Gruyère cheese:
A variety of Swiss cheese with a firm, smooth texture, small holes, and a strong, tangy flavor; great for snacking or cooking.

Guava:
A round tropical fruit with a yellow skin and pink inner flesh and many seeds. Grown commercially in Hawai'i. The purée or juice is available as a frozen concentrate. Guava can also be made into jams, jellies, and sauces.

L

Liliko'i:
A common variety of this fruit in Hawai'i has a yellow, shiny outer shell filled inside with seeds surrounded with a juicy pulp. This juice is tangy and unique in flavor. It is also known as passion fruit.

M

Macadamia nuts:
Rich, oily nut grown mostly on the Big Island of Hawai'i. Also called "mac nuts."

Mahimahi:
  Also called dolphinfish, with a firm, pink flesh. Best fresh but often available frozen. A standard in island restaurants and markets. Substitute snapper, catfish, or halibut.

Mango:
  Gold and green tropical fruit available in many supermarkets. Available fresh June through September in Hawai'i.

Maui onion:
  A very sweet, juicy, large round onion similar to the Vidalia or Walla Walla onion. Often available on the West Coast but expensive. Substitute any sweet white onion.

Mirin:
  Sweet Japanese rice wine.

Mochiko:
  Japanese glutinous rice flour used in making pastries and some sauces.

O

Ono:
  A mackerel with white, firm flesh. Also known as wahoo. Substitute tuna, swordfish, or shark.

Opah:
  A very large moonfish. Substitute swordfish.

Oyster sauce:
  A concentrated sauce made from oyster juice and salt, used in many Chinese and other Asian dishes to impart a full, rich flavor.

P

Panko:
  A crispy, large-flaked Japanese bread crumb that adds more texture than ordinary bread crumbs. Found in Asian markets.

Papaya:
  A tropical fruit with yellow flesh, black seeds, and a perfumy scent. The most common papaya eaten in Hawai'i is the solo papaya. Other types may be larger or have pink flesh; all are suitable for island recipes.

Phyllo pastry:
  Thin layers of dough used to make pastries, originating from Mediterranean cuisine. The Greek word *phyllon* literally means "leaf."

Poi:
  A starchy paste made by pounding taro root with water until it reaches a smooth consistency. A staple in traditional Hawaiian diet.

S

Sake:
    Clear Japanese rice wine. Other strong clear liquors such as tequila or vodka can be substituted.

Shiitake mushroom:
    The second most widely cultivated mushroom in the world, medium to large with umbrella-shaped, flopped tan to dark brown caps with edges that tend to roll under. Shiitakes have a woodsy, smoky flavor. Can be purchased fresh or dried in Asian groceries. To reconstitute the dried variety, soak in warm water for 30 minutes before using. Stem both fresh and dried shiitakes.

Soy sauce:
    A dark salty liquid made from soybeans, flour, salt, and water. Dark soy sauce is stronger than light soy sauce. A staple in most Asian cuisines. Also called shoyu.

Sweet vermouth:
    A fortified wine aperitif flavored with herbs, spices, barks, and flowers. Various brands of vermouth are produced in both Italy and France, and flavors can be added through infusion, maceration, or distillation. The original version of Vermouth used in cocktails was from Italy, and is what we often refer to as sweet vermouth today.

T

Tapioca:
    A starchy substance derived from the root of the cassava plant that is used as a thickening agent for soups, fruit fillings, and desserts. Used much like cornstarch.

Taro:
    A starchy root of the taro, called kalo, is pounded to make poi. Its flavor is similar to artichokes or chestnuts. The leaves (lūʻau) and stems (hāhā) are also used in cooking. Taro contains an irritating substance and must be cooked before any part of the plant can be eaten.